*I wish you understanding —
of how special you really are; a
journey, safe from the storms and
warmed by the sun; a path to
wonderful things; an invitation, to
the abundance life brings; and a smile
in your heart, for all the days to come.*

— Douglas Pagels

Other Titles in This Series:

223 Great Things About Mothers

223 Great Things About Sisters

223 Great Things Teens Should Do

Library of Congress Control Number: 2008909621
ISBN: 978-1-59842-363-1

�oand Blue Mountain Press are registered in U.S. Patent and Trademark Office. Certain trademarks are used under license.

Printed in China.
First Printing: 2009

✺ This book is printed on recycled paper.

This book is printed on fine quality, laid embossed, 80 lb. paper. This paper has been specially produced to be acid free (neutral pH) and contains no groundwood or unbleached pulp. It conforms with the requirements of the American National Standards Institute, Inc., so as to ensure that this book will last and be enjoyed by future generations.

Blue Mountain Arts, Inc.
P.O. Box 4549, Boulder, Colorado 80306

223

Great Things to

Always

REMEMBER

Douglas Pagels

Blue Mountain Press™

Boulder, Colorado

Great Things to
Always
REMEMBER...

⇐ As you go through the days of
the year ahead, busy with all the
responsibilities the world has placed
upon you, remember to keep the
truly special things in mind.

⇐ Live to the fullest and make
each day count.

⇐ Have happiness as one of
your priorities!

↤ Remember to keep things
in perspective.

↤ Be creative and aware and
wonderfully alive.

↤ Take those long walks that
would love to be taken.

↤ Don't let the important things
go unsaid.

↩ Always remember where to find your smile.

↩ Have the faith it takes to achieve and aspire.

↩ New journeys await you in the days to come.

↩ May your tomorrows take you to the summit of your goals.

↩ And may your joys take you even higher.

← Slow down and enjoy the view.

　　← It's important to get headed
　　in the right direction...

← But don't get so caught up in your
destination that you forget to delight
in the scenery of each new day.

　　← Remember that some of the
　　secret joys of living are not
　　found by rushing from point
　　A to point B...

← But by slowing down and inventing
some imaginary letters along the way.

Don't just have minutes in the day.

Have moments in time.

← Your presence is a present
to the world.

← Everything about you is unique;
you're one of a kind.

← Your life can be what you
want it to be.

← Take the days just one at a time.

← Count your blessings, not
  your troubles.

← You'll make it through whatever
  comes along.

← Within you are so many answers.

← Understand, have courage,
  be strong.

*You have so many treasures within —
those you're only beginning to discover and
all the ones you're already aware of.*

*Never forget what a wonder you are. That
special person in the mirror may not
always get to hear all the compliments you
deserve, but you are so worthy of such an
abundance... of friendship, joy, and love.*

⤺ Don't put limits on yourself.

⤺ So many dreams are
waiting to be realized.

⤺ Decisions are too important
to leave to chance.

⤺ Reach for your peak,
your goal, your prize.

∈ Nothing wastes more energy
than worrying.

∈ The longer one carries a problem,
the heavier it gets.

∈ Don't take things too seriously.

∈ Live a life of serenity, not a life
of regrets.

← Realize that it's never too late.

← Do ordinary things in an extraordinary way.

← Have health and hope and happiness.

← Take the time to wish upon a star.

← And don't ever forget — for even a day — how very special you are.

The darkest hour is the best
time to see the stars.

You'll find that optimism is
very refreshing.

The wisest people on earth
are those who have a hard
time recalling their worries...

And an easy time remembering
their blessings.

*A life well lived is simply
a compilation of days well spent.

⇐ Follow your hopes and dreams while you're still young (or young at heart)!

⇐ Take advantage of your chances.

⇐ Don't be a ship that stays in the harbor, never straying from its safety.

⇐ Don't spend your whole life waiting for a perfect moment that may never come along.

⤺ If you really want to do it,
do it while you can.

⤺ Make a plan, carry it out,
and pursue it with all your heart.

⤺ Be brave... and sail away.

⤺ And one of these days, send the
rest of us a postcard saying how
beautiful those hopes and dreams
turned out to be.

Sometimes it's important to work for that pot of gold. But other times it's essential to take time off and to make sure that your most important decision in the day simply consists of choosing which color to slide down on the rainbow.

≤ Smile inside about all the good things you do.

 ≤ Even when no one else is singing your praises, give yourself permission to sing all you want.

≤ Admire your accomplishments!

 ≤ Large or small, tremendous or tiny, they contribute to the well-being of this world.

≤ A little light somewhere makes a brighter light everywhere. And your contribution does more good than you know.

← I may be uncertain about exactly where I'm headed, but I am very clear regarding this: I'm glad I've got a ticket to go on this magnificent journey.

← I hope you are, too.

← Don't be afraid to explore unfamiliar territory.

← If you do happen to get lost, you may stumble across some of the most interesting discoveries you'll ever make.

↜ Wander down roads you've never taken before.

↜ Get off the beaten path.

↜ Check out things you'll never chance upon again.

↜ And remember: life isn't a travel guide to follow...

↜ It's an adventure to undertake.

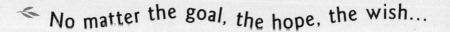 No matter the goal, the hope, the wish...

you can find the courage to do it.

↤ I want you to know… you're an original.

↤ An individual.

↤ A masterpiece.

↤ Celebrate that!

↤ Don't be shy.

↤ And don't ever feel like
you should be someone
other than who you are.

↤ Every star is important to the sky.

≪ Enjoy the little things.

≪ The precious moments.

≪ The priceless memories.

≪ Your most cherished thoughts.

≪ The images of special faces and meaningful places.

≪ Time can't take away anything that has already been given.

↢ Your treasures from days gone by are treasures still.

↢ Happiness is not one big, beautiful jewel we can hold — or lose — in our hands.

↢ Each one of us is an hourglass.

↢ And in the course of our lives, we get to keep the diamonds that come our way among the passing sands.

I hope that the distance between where you are and where you want to be grows shorter every day.

I hope you will be touched by kindness.

I hope you will be inspired by wisdom.

I hope you will be graced with understanding.

And I hope that every one of your days will dawn with something to be grateful for, some special dream to reach for, and someone who lights up your life.

When you do the things you do with love...

you give life a gleam that most people
only carry a glimpse of.

⬱ Don't ever try to understand everything; some things will just never make sense.

⬱ Don't ever be afraid to try to make things better; you might be surprised at the results.

⬱ Don't ever feel threatened by the future; enjoy life one day at a time.

⬱ Don't ever feel guilty about the past; simply learn from any mistakes that were made.

← Don't ever feel that you are alone;
   there is always somebody there for
   you to reach out to.

← Don't ever forget that you can achieve
   so many of the things you can imagine;
   it's not as hard as it seems.

← Don't ever stop loving.

← Don't ever stop believing.

← Don't ever stop dreaming your dreams.

Gardeners will tell you that the best time to plant a tree was years ago, and the second best time... is now. There's something you need to know before continuing on with the rest of your life. The same philosophy that applies to trees also holds true for personal goals. Imagine this...

On this very day, even one year ago, if you had started a plan to reach a new goal, think how far along you'd be! The best time to plant those seeds, follow those dreams, and start reaching for the sky... was back then.

The second best time to begin... is now.

Spend today walking away from worry and move toward serenity.

Leave behind conflict and travel toward solutions.

Make your present happier and your path smoother.

And best of all? You'll be taking a step into a beautiful future.

≼ In all of our days, our lives are
always changing.

≼ Tears come along as well as smiles.

≼ Along the roads you travel, may
the miles be a thousand times
more lovely than lonely.

≼ May they give you gifts that never
ever end.

➤ May you have someone
   wonderful to love.

➤ A dear friend in whom you
   can confide.

➤ May you have rainbows after
   every storm.

➤ May you have hopes to keep
   you warm.

➤ And may you always have
   an angel by your side.

Be the kind of person...

who doesn't make your guardian angel
work too hard or worry too much.

↜ Sometimes the paths we take
are long and hard, but those
are usually the ones that lead
to the most beautiful views.

↜ Challenges always
come along.

↜ How you respond to them
determines who you are deep
down inside and everything
you're going to be.

↜ Increase the chances of
reaching your goals by
working at them gradually.

↞ Go out of your way to be good
to an older person.

↞ You'll discover that you can make
somebody's entire day with a smile,
a phone call, some fresh-picked
daisies, or whatever it is you've got.

↢ Our elders have so much to give
  to those who listen.

↢ But they are the ones who deserve
  to receive.

↢ Don't pass up the chance to brighten
  their lives.

↢ An old adage reminds us that they
  need only a little.

↢ But they need that little... a lot.

If you can reach out, you can make it happen.

If you just begin, you can continue.

If you can strive, you can climb even higher.

If you don't put limits on yourself, you can discover the amazing things you can do.

If you keep planting
the seeds of your dreams...

they'll do their best
to blossom for you.

← Don't let worries get in the way of recognizing how great things can be.

← Always keep moving ahead.

← Balance out any bad that is going on in the world with any good you can provide.

← When you leave behind all that
  has been, you are on the way to
  all that can be.

← Sometimes you just have to be
  patient and brave and strong.

← If you don't know how, just make
  it up as you go along.

I want your life to be such a wonderful one. I wish you peace, deep within your soul; joyfulness in the promise of each new day; stars to reach for, dreams to come true, and memories more beautiful than words can say.

I wish you friends close at heart, even over the miles; loved ones — the best treasures we're blessed with; present moments to live in, one day at a time; serenity, with its wisdom; courage, with its strength; and new beginnings, to give life a chance to really shine.

🌿 When a new beginning unfolds in the story of your life, wonderful things can come into view.

🌿 New promises can be made.

🌿 New commitments can be kept.

🌿 Today is a brand-new gift.

🌿 Untie the ribbons and bows, and let today show you how positive a new beginning can be.

← When people aren't giving you the credit you deserve, don't let their lack of recognition make you feel like any less of a wonderful person.

← Just do what you need to do to keep your inner light shining.

← Stay positive.

← You know who you are.

← You know how much you do and how deeply you care.

↤ Remember all the good things you've done to grace the days of those around you.

↤ And when it seems like you're getting overlooked and underappreciated, find reassurance and comfort in quietly saying this:

↤ "I am aware that I am less than some people prefer me to be, but most people are unaware that I am so much more than what they see."

Good friends are hard to find.

Good friends are easy
to love.

Good friends are presents that
last forever and that feel like gifts
from above.

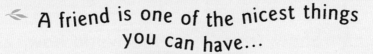 A friend is one of the nicest things
you can have...

and one of the best things you can be.

← Hold on to your dreams and never let them go.

← Show the rest of the world how wonderful you are!

← Make the most of your days and remember... they're far too precious to let them slip away.

≼ Give circumstances a chance.

≼ Give others the benefit of
the doubt.

≼ Rely on all the strength you
have inside.

≼ Take on your problems one by
one and work things out.

Even if you can't just snap your fingers and make a dream come true, you can travel in the direction of your dream, every single day, and you can keep shortening the distance between the two of you.

🌿 Stay in touch with those who touch your life with love.

🌿 Look on the bright side.

🌿 Remember that your special qualities will always see you through.

🌿 Keep your spirits up.

🌿 Make your heart happy... and let it reflect on everything you do!

- Make tomorrow happier by going there in ways that really matter.
- Decisions lie ahead, wondering... what will you do?
- Where will you go?
- How will you choose when the choices are yours?

↜ Remember that bad choices can come back to haunt you.

↜ Remember that good choices come back to bless you, over and over again.

↜ Work for the ability to choose wisely, to prosper, to succeed.

There are times when just being brave
is all you need to be.

☙ Remember that it's up to you to find the key that unlocks the door to your happiness.

☙ Discover how to get closer and closer to a more fulfilling life.

☙ Get rid of the "if only's."

☙ And get on with whatever you need to do... to get things right.

← Life throws curves at us from time to time.

← You can't always control what happens, but you can control how you deal with it.

← Stay positive, stay in touch, reach out, and keep the faith.

↞ Be patient and let the story
  unfold a page at a time.

↞ Brighter days come from
  doing constructive, creative,
  caring things...

↞ And from just being strong until
  the tide turns.

☙ Hope can bring you peaceful moments when the world around you is difficult to comprehend.

☙ Hope is a comforting reminder that tomorrow will be here soon, ready to give us a fresh, new start.

☙ Hope is the warm and welcomed knowledge that beautiful possibilities exist.

☙ Hope is all these special things and in simply knowing this: when hope is all you've got... you've still got a lot.

Even if you can't change the world...

never doubt that you can do remarkable
things to change and rearrange
your little corner of it.

← You have everything you need
to take you where you want
to go.

← You have abilities and attributes
that belong to you alone.

← You have qualities that get better
every day.

← You have courage and strength to
see you through.

↞ You have gifts that have never even been opened.

↞ You are a special person, and you have a future that is in the best of hands.

↞ And you need to remember: if you have plans you want to act on and dreams you've always wanted to come true... you have what it takes.

↞ Because you... have you.

I Wish for You...

Happiness. Deep down within.
Serenity. With each sunrise.
Success. In each facet of your life.
Close and caring friends.
Love. That never ends.

Special memories. Of all the yesterdays.
A bright today. With much to be thankful for.
A path. That leads to beautiful tomorrows.

Dreams. That do their best to come true.
And appreciation. Of all the wonderful
things about you.

✒ Be creative.

✒ You're the artist here.

✒ You're the one who can brush away the clouds and make the sun shine.

✒ Paint your own picture.

✒ Choose your own colors.

✒ And forget all that business about having to stay between the lines.

- You are someone with such
  great potential!

- You have the ability to make
  every day special.

- Each new morning comes to
  us gift-wrapped.

- Fresh out of the box are chances
  we've never taken and opportunities
  we've never known.

← Those with the "same old, same old" outlook let the golden moments just slip away.

← But those who understand the value of the gift?

← They have the chance to turn the present into a truly extraordinary day!

⬳ Appreciate, with all your heart,
the best of life.

     ⬳ Do everything within your
power to pass the tests
of life.

⬳ And learn how to live with the rest
of life.

Don't forget: you're in the driver's seat...

and you can travel through life
in any direction you choose.

← You are such a wonder.

← You're the only one in the universe exactly like you!

← I want you to take care of that rare and remarkable soul.

← I want you to know that there is someone who will thank you for doing the things you do now with foresight and wisdom and respect.

← It's the person you will someday be.

↤ You have a chance to make
that person so thankful and proud.

↤ It's so important that you take the
time to choose wisely every time
you're given the chance.

↤ Choose to do the things that
reflect well... on your ability,
your integrity, your spirit, your
health, your tomorrows, your
smiles, your dreams, and yourself.

✑ Each day brings with it the
miracle of a new beginning.

✑ Many of the moments ahead will be
marvelously disguised as ordinary days...

✑ But each one of us has the chance to
make something extraordinary out of them.